KIDS IN CRISIS

KIDS
&
MEDIA
INFLUENCE

Cynthia DiLaura Devore, M.D.

DEDICATION

*To CMD, MJD, and APD, with love
and gratitude for your support.*

6920821

Published by Abdo & Daughters, 4940 Viking Drive, Suite 622, Edina, Minnesota 55435.

Library bound edition distributed by Rockbottom Books, Pentagon Tower, P.O. Box 36036, Minneapolis, Minnesota 55435.

Printed in the United States.

Cover Photo credit: Bettmann
Interior Photo credits: Wide World

Edited By Rosemary Wallner

Library of Congress Cataloging-in-Publication Data

Devore, Cynthia DiLaura, 1947-
    Kids and media influence / by Cynthia DiLaura Devore.
        p.   cm. -- (Kids in crisis)
    Includes bibliographical references and index.
    ISBN 1-56239-324-3
    1. Television and children--United States--Juvenile literature.
    2. Mass media and children--United States--Juvenile literature.
    3. Violence in television--United States--Juvenile literature.
    [1. Violence in television.   2. Television--Psychological aspects.]
    I. Title.   II. Series.
    HQ784.T4D528   1994
    305.23'083--dc20   94-25562
                                                 CIP
                                               AC

CONTENTS

1

NOTE TO PARENTS AND TEACHERS

Parents and teachers have an extraordinary task. They must try to nurture and guide children to become productive, happy adults in a world full of increasing dangers. Drugs and guns are widespread. Violence is glamorized on television and is rampant in the streets. Values are distorted. These are difficult times to be a child. These are also difficult times to be a parent or teacher.

This series is intended to help us keep our children safe in the midst of all this turmoil. The stories and exercises can accomplish this in part by helping young adults to develop their own skills at making thoughtful, critical decisions. Each book in the Kids in Crisis series begins with a story (based on a true incident) that illustrates each problem. The story presents children in grades five through seven with a reality-based approach to each topic.

Television became a powerful medium in the 1950s. The photo above shows a child tuning in his television which is placed in the fireplace.

The narrative is also meant to be instructional. The course of decision-making is mapped out as the story unfolds in a step-wise cumulative fashion building on the choices made by the children in the stories.

In *Kids & Media Influence*, the profile story is about a young boy who watched an adult cartoon and acted out the theme, resulting in harm to his sister. The story is true and provides students with a slightly different perspective on what they see on television. The primary media of focus in this book is television. TV is the primary vehicle used in American households today for information and entertainment. However, the book can lead to a discussion of how other media, including literature, radio, and music, can also influence them.

The next chapter discusses choices and consequences, with references directly back to the profile story. This provides an opportunity to discuss alternative choices. It also introduces the concept of impulsive versus thoughtful actions and accountability for choices.

The third chapter presents facts and statistics about media in a nonjudgmental fashion. This allows the reader to become better informed and thereby better able to develop critical thinking skills.

The next two chapters present the case for and against controlling the media. The focus is mostly on television violence, but other health influences of television, such as alcohol use, obesity, and sexuality, are also mentioned. Again, facts are presented so that students are encouraged to draw their own conclusions.

The sixth chapter returns to the profile story with a look at values that emerged as the incident unfolded. Strong values are the key to a healthy journey through adolescence. Unfortunately, the trend of television programming has been to undermine many traditional American values.

Finally in "Your Turn," students have their turn to complete projects or think about and discuss issues that they may have garnered from the book.

Each book in the series should serve as a springboard for discussion between young people and their grown-ups. Ultimately, the more we communicate with our children at any level, the better equipped they will be to handle life's difficult choices when we may not be around to help them.

Your thoughts and comments on this topic or ideas for future topics are most welcome. The author, like you, is dedicated to the well-being of our children. Please address your comments to the author in care of the publisher.

2

JOHN AND JULIE'S STORY

This story is based on a true incident of a young boy and his sister. Circumstances have been changed to protect the identity of the family.

John was five years old. He lived in a trailer with his mother and father and his two-year-old sister, Julie. John was a very active boy. He loved to play. But the thing he liked to do best was to watch television. He enjoyed cartoons the most.

His parents did not have much money. They each worked two jobs. They were often tired. On many nights John watched television while his parents slept or worked. His mother joked that the television was John's favorite baby-sitter.

One night John was changing channels looking for a cartoon show. But John found that not too many cartoons were on television at night. Most of the programs he found were for adults. He did not like any of them. Suddenly, he found a cartoon show he had never seen before. It was on a music channel teenagers usually watch.

The cartoon was about a teenager named Loudmouth. Loudmouth said some nasty things about grown-ups. He made fun of them. As a matter of fact, he made fun of almost everything. He used rude words. John knew these words would get him into trouble if his mother or father heard him say them. Yet, it was funny to hear these words on television. John laughed.

Every night John found Loudmouth on television at the same time. He started to say the words he heard Loudmouth use. At first, John was careful not to use the words in front of his parents. Loudmouth had shown him how to trick parents. Loudmouth could get away with doing bad things and never get caught. John figured he could, too. John liked Loudmouth so much he started to pretend he was Loudmouth. He even started using Loudmouth's bad language, especially with his little sister.

His parents began to notice a change in John's behavior. They did not know what had caused him to become so rude and mean. They decided he was just going through a stage and told him to stop. Mostly, though, John's parents ignored his bad behavior.

Loudmouth had a younger sister, just like John. Loudmouth's sister's name was Barbara, but he called her Bad Breath. Loudmouth called his sister other bad names, too. He treated her poorly and laughed when he made her cry. John laughed, too. He thought the names Loudmouth called his sister were funny. He began to call his own sister some of the same words. When she head the words, Julie would cry. When his parents heard the words, John got into trouble. They told him these words were not appropriate and that they did not want to hear him use them. Many times, though, they did not know what he was doing. They were too busy. John pretended more and more to be like Loudmouth. It was fun.

One night when Loudmouth got mad at his sister, he took a match and set her bed on fire. Loudmouth set fire to many things he did not like. John laughed.

That night after watching Loudmouth, John went to the drawer where his mother kept a cigarette lighter. He knew he was not supposed to touch it. But Loudmouth used lighters, and it was okay for him. So John did, too. He was only pretending, he thought.

John went into Julie's room. She was asleep in her bed. John said some mean words to her, just like he heard Loudmouth do to Bad Breath. Julie did not wake up. John lit the cigarette lighter. He remembered his mother telling him never to play with fire. He stopped for a moment and looked at the flame. Then he held the lighter to the corner of his sister's blanket. He laughed a nasty little laugh, just like Loudmouth did when he set his sister's bed on fire. John saw the blanket start to smoke. He turned off the lighter. Then John left Julie's room and went back to watch another program on television.

Soon he fell asleep on the sofa. He woke up when he heard his mother calling him. He could not see her. He was having trouble breathing. The entire trailer was filled with thick dark smoke. He was scared and called for his parents. He felt his father's strong arms lift him up. His father carried him outside. He felt the cool night air fill his lungs. He could breathe again. He was safe.

His mother came from the trailer. Thick black smoke poured out the door. She was crying. She had tried to go to Julie's room, but flames drove her away. She cried and cried.

The fire trucks came. It took hours to put out the fire. John and his parents sat in a neighbor's trailer watching from the window. Their trailer had burned to the ground. There was nothing left. Julie was lost in the rubble. John felt numb.

John suddenly realized what had really happened. He remembered Loudmouth. He remembered the lighter. Loudmouth's fires never burned down his house. It was just for fun. What happened? He wondered what had gone wrong.

John heard the fire chief talk to his parents. The fire chief asked if John had been playing with matches. John heard his mother crying. He saw the burned trailer. He remembered his little sister. He was scared and sad. He started to cry. He went up to his parents and told them what had happened. "I didn't mean to hurt Julie, Mommy," he sobbed. "It was just a joke, like in Loudmouth. I didn't know the trailer would burn down."

John and his family are still trying to recover from their tragedy. Their lives will never be the same. John's parents decided that they can help other parents to understand the influence television can have on children by sharing their sad story.

"Tom and Jerry" has entertained children for over 30 years. It was one of the first cartoons to utilize slapstick-like humor.

3

CHOICES AND CONSEQUENCES

A choice is the act of selecting one thing or behavior over another. A consequence is the outcome or result of the choice made. Every choice has a consequence. Some choices are good, and some consequences are good. Other choices are poor, and the consequences are bad. Sometimes people cannot always control things that happen to them. For example, John's parents did not have much money. They each had to work two jobs to support their family. They were often tired.

They were not around to supervise their children. They chose to take the risk of leaving their children unsupervised for long periods of time. They chose to let John watch as much television as he wanted. They did not help him select programs. They allowed him to stay up late and watch television shows that were not appropriate for young children. Yet they never asked him what he was watching. John spent so much time alone that his parents did not even know what adult shows he was watching.

John's parents chose not to ask him how he was spending his time. They did not talk with him and teach him that the things he saw on television were not always true.

They left him alone to make decisions about important things. When they noticed a change in his behavior, they shrugged it off as just a stage of life. They did not find out the cause of the changes or to try and stop them. They did not correct his bad behaviors.

They also left a cigarette lighter in a place where John could find it. Not only was John left unsupervised, but he was also left alone in a dangerous setting. So was Julie.

*Many families today allow the television to
be their children's baby-sitter.*

Choices that parents make, especially parents with young children, affect their children. One horrible consequence of John's parents' choice to let the television be John's baby-sitter was the loss of their daughter. Another consequence is that John's life will be affected forever. He has to confront his role in his sister's death. That is a heavy burden for anyone.

John was too young to be held completely responsible for his act. However, John made choices he knew were wrong. He knew the words that Loudmouth said were unacceptable. Yet he chose to use them. He knew it was wrong to be mean to his sister, but he did it because it was funny. He knew he was not allowed to touch lighters, but he did. He knew he was not supposed to play with fire, but he did.

A five-year-old may not be able to separate the real world from the pretend. John probably did not understand that on television things he saw were not real. He did not see Loudmouth's house burn down after Loudmouth set fire to his sister's bed. Loudmouth's sister was not shown hurt from the fire. John did not think those things would happen to him. He still had to realize the consequences.

The story of John and Julie had a very sad outcome. It leaves the reader wondering whether anything could have been done to prevent that family's sorrow.

4

MEDIA FACTS AND STATISTICS

In the 1920s General Electric sold the first television sets. The screens were no bigger than the palm of the hand. At that time the only programs offered were occasional test broadcasts. Only people who were very rich or curious bought the new invention.

In the 1930s the three major networks—ABC, CBS, and NBC—were established. NBC aired its first program, a variety show called "Hour Glass," on July 7, 1936. None of the networks had many shows to put on the air, however. NBC showed about 15 hours of programming per week. As in the 1920s, no one wanted to buy the expensive TV sets because there was nothing to watch. By the early 1940s, RCA had sold only about ten thousand sets.

By 1948 however, networks were airing more and more shows, including "Texaco Star Theater," "Howdy Doody" and "Kukla, Fran and Ollie."

By 1952 the first TV commercials appeared. In 1959 more shows for young people appeared. One study done at that time said that teenagers were spending up to five hours a day watching TV. As the technology increased in the 1950s, the black-and-white images became color ones. Sports games, news shows, and more and more comedy shows were added to the network's programming.

Today American children watch three to five hours of television per day—a statistic not too far off from the study completed in 1959. By the time the average American youngster is six, they will spend more time watching TV than they will spend talking to their father in a lifetime. By age 16, the average American will have watched 18,000 hours of television. By high school graduation the average teenager will have spent about 22,000 hours watching television. That is more time watching TV than they will have spent in the classroom learning for all their years of education.

Violence on television has been around since its inception. The above photograph is from a 1960 episode of "The Untouchables," reenacting the attempted assassination of President Franklin D. Roosevelt.

Fred Dryer in the television show "Hunter." Dryer portrayed a cop who often used violent means to apprehend violent criminals.

What does a growing child see during these hours of television viewing? The average child sees 12,000 violent acts every year on television. By the age of 16 the average teenager has seen 200,000 acts of violence on the screen.

In 1982 there were one-and-a-half hours of war cartoons on TV weekly. In 1986 there were 43 hours of war cartoons weekly. In war cartoons there are about 48 violent acts per hour, with murder or attempted murder occurring almost once every minute. The rate of violence in children's programs is three times greater than the rate of violence in adult programs.

Over a thousand scientific studies have linked heavy exposure to TV violence to aggressive behavior in children. The more children see violence, the more they use violence to resolve disputes.

In 1973 a small town in Canada was wired for the first time for television. By 1975 hitting, biting, and shoving among first and second graders increased 160 percent.

As violence in television programming increased in the 1980s, there was a significant increase in childhood violent crimes in the United States. Juvenile arrests for murder jumped 85 percent between 1987 and 1991. Between 1988 and 1990 children less than 18 were responsible for 70 percent of all hate crimes in the United States. Between 1988 and 1990 rape arrests for 13-year-old boys increased 200 percent. Most violence on TV is against women.

Through commercials, advertisers use television to promote their products. About $700 million per year is spent on advertising directed at children. The average American child sees more than 20,000 commercials each year on television.

Approximately 60 percent of all that advertising is for food. During children viewing hours, 96 percent of all food ads are for high-calorie, high-fat foods, like fast foods and junk foods, presweetened cereals, and candy. Only 4 percent of all food ads are for milk, meat, bread, and juice.

In addition to commercials about food, people on television programs eat, talk about, or handle food about eight times per hour. Watching people eat can make the viewer want to eat.

Television viewing is known to decrease physical activity in children. The combination of a decrease in physical activity and an increase in eating causes weight gain. Between 1971 and 1981 the problem of obesity in children steadily increased. Today children in the United States are in poorer physical condition than their parents were at the same age.

Although advertising of hard liquor is prohibited on television, wine and beer ads are allowed. Studies of these ads have revealed that more bottles and glasses are shown than characters in the ads. Only 1 percent of all ads ever show a person drunk. The combination of a lot of glasses and bottles without intoxication (drunkenness) misleads the watcher. It gives the viewer the message that people can drink wine and beer in large quantities without getting drunk.

Nighttime drama programs average almost five mentions or displays of alcohol use per hour. Daytime soap operas average six alcohol scenes per hour. Research has shown that children model behaviors they see. In 1980, 6.11 million Americans over the age of two watched at least 15 minutes of soap operas on any one afternoon. In 1991, 88 percent of American teenagers in grades nine through twelve had tried alcohol. Of those, 43 percent had more than five drinks at on sitting, meaning they drank to get drunk.

American teenagers view nearly 14,000 sexual suggestions per year. Only 150 of those 14,000 suggestions talk about birth control, self-control, or abstinence. The sexual content of soap operas has increased by 103 percent since 1980. Between 1981 and 1991 the pregnancy rate among 15-year-olds and younger has steadily increased.

Suicide accounts for about 8 percent of all deaths in teens. In 1986 after the first of four made-for-TV films about suicide, suicide attempts and successful completions more than doubled among teenagers in New York City.

5

THE CASE FOR CONTROLLING THE MEDIA

Television, radio, and printed words are generally believed to be the world's most powerful means of communication.

An episode of "Happy Days" showed Henry Winkler's character, Fonzie, applying for a library card. The next day, there was a huge increase in the number of children applying for library cards in the United States.

Scientists have completed many studies about television's effects on viewers. In 1991 Drs. William Dietz and Victor Strasburger completed their study. They reviewed the effects of television on children and young adults. They found that television influences many health behaviors. These behaviors include the use of drugs and other substances, physical fitness, sex, suicide, and violence. The doctors asked broadcasters to create programs that meet the needs of children and young adults. The doctors felt that the government should regulate programming.

A psychologist from the University of Chicago studied television viewers for 22 years. Dr. Leonard D. Efrom studied 400 people watching television. He concluded that watching television can affect someone's behavior. "There can no longer be any doubt," Efrom wrote, "that heavy exposure to televised violence is one the causes of aggressive behavior, crime and violence in society."

How does television affect a viewer's attitude toward violence? Dr. David Pearl of the National Institute of Mental Health found one answer. He said that television tells people how to be violent. Because viewers watch so many violent acts on TV, they become less sensitive to these acts. They see violence as a normal and accepted way of life. When viewers leave the television, they use violence often and more quickly in their lives.

Dr. Frank M. Palumbo, a pediatrician, had some strong words to describe the violence that appears on TV. He said this violence was a "toxic substance in the environment that is harmful to children." In 1988 he was outraged at Congressman Peter Rodino for Rodino's views on controlling the media. Rodino said that he wanted the government to protect commerce more than he wanted to protect children.

What does the U.S. Constitution say about controlling the media? The First Amendment guarantees free speech to everyone. That means people are free to write and say what they want. But Judge Robert H. Bork, former judge of the U.S. Court of Appeals, thinks there should be some control. He said that the First Amendment was never meant to mean a complete lack of government control. He pointed out that people can be arrested for shouting swear words in public. Shouldn't the media, Bork added, have some guidelines about the swearing and violence it provides to the public?

Tipper Gore is the former president of the Parents' Music Resource Center. She is also the wife of Vice President Albert Gore. She admitted that rap and rock music lyrics were not the only cause of the rise in youth crime. However, she added, "certainly kids are

Judge Robert Bork, former judge of the U.S. Court of Appeals, believes there should be some government control over network television.

Tipper Gore, wife of Vice President Al Gore and President of the Parents' Music Resource Center, is heading up a crusade to give government more control over the recording and television industry.

influenced by the glorification of violence." Along with researchers, she asked the government for more media regulation.

In 1989 Gilda Berger wrote a book about the media and violence. She pointed out that Sweden and New Zealand have stricter controls on the media than in the United States. The government's increased control, she said, did not cause the loss of other freedoms for the people.

Drs. James Dobson and Gary L. Baurer wrote a book called Children at Risk. They pointed out that television programs do not portray real life, although children may think they do. One study showed that 55 percent of prime-time television contained violence. In real life that figure would be less than 1 percent. They wrote that companies in the United States can make any movie they want to. But should movies mock American values?

The authors are also concerned that television uses obscene language during family viewing time and shows programs that are anti-tradition, anti-religion, and anti-family. A tradition is a belief or practice handed down from one generation to the next. Traditions include values that a community sees as important to protect. The authors believe that mocking traditions and values attacks many Americans. It teaches children not to trust basic beliefs their parents may be trying to teach them. They point out that the best and most powerful tool is the off button on the television.

Actress Lucille Ball once talked about how much television had changed over the years. When she was expecting her first child in the 1950s, she and her husband were starring in the TV program "I Love Lucy." Ball said that the writers wrote the real pregnancy into the script. The characters of Lucy and Ricky, however, were not allowed to use the word "pregnant" on the air. They had to say Lucy was "in the family way." The beds in Lucy and Ricky's TV bedroom had to be separate twin beds pushed together. Sheets and blankets had to be separate. The two characters could not be in the same bed together.

*Lucille Ball starred in the 1950s TV show, "I Love Lucy."
She appeared on the show pregnant, but the word was
never used. She and her TV husband, who was also her
husband in real-life, had separate beds on the show.*

Ball said that in today's television programming writers and studio executives think differently. "Now they not only use the word 'pregnant,'" Ball said, "they show you how she got that way." Ball questioned whether it was really needed. She suggested that there may be some middle ground that was not too uptight or too loose, but would still entertain.

In 1990 Senator Paul Simon asked television executives from all stations to get together and develop better self-controls to monitor programs. The executives answered that laws needed to be changed to allow them to get together to control the airways. Simon pushed a temporary law through Congress to see if the executives would follow through on their promise to regulate themselves. By mid 1991, nothing had changed.

Simon angrily spoke against the television industry's promise to control itself. Simon hopes that the government's threat to set controls on the television industry will pressure TV executives to change. He feels that without this threat, executives have shown that they do not monitor themselves.

Finally, people for better controls on the media point out that television can be a teacher for many. They say a classroom teacher is not allowed to use foul language and violence. A teacher would be fired for mocking family values. Why then are there not similar controls on TV?

6

THE CASE AGAINST CONTROLLING THE MEDIA

The First Amendment to the U.S. Constitution guarantees the freedom of speech and the press. Supreme Court Justice William O. Douglas wrote that courts and legislatures must not violate that freedom; that freedom of expression, even if it's full of sex and violence, should not be controlled. Other prominent people have given their reasons for not controlling the media's freedom of speech

Dr. Robert Brustein, a drama professor at Harvard University, believes that violent films do not cause violence. He feels they just reflect violence that is always present in every society.

Steven Bochco, a producer of successful television shows, feels it is his job as a producer to test the limits of what can be shown on television. He calls himself an "equal opportunity offender."

Steven Bochco, Emmy Award-winning television producer, is a staunch advocate for freedom of expression. He is against any government regulation on the TV industry.

*Jack Valenti, president of the Motion Picture Association of America,
prepares to testify on Capitol Hill before the Senate Judiciary subcommittee
on the Constitution which was holding hearings on television violence.
Valenti is a supporter of freedom of expression.*

In 1993 Alfred R. Schneider of ABC television said that his network's policy controlled the use of violence. Outside monitoring by the government was not needed. ABC's policy states that TV programs only use violence if it "reasonably" adds to the story. Schneider, like most other leaders in the film and television industries, feels that he does monitor his programs.

In December 1993 two companies that made assault-filled video games voluntarily took two games off the market in response to public pressure. This is an example of how media industries monitor themselves.

Supporters of the free speech part of the First Amendment also argue that people have the right to see what they want to see. The supporters say that people do not have to go to movies they do not want to see. The supporters say that Americans like to see violence in films. Violent films make more money than nonviolent films.

People against controlling the media believe that parents have the responsibility to protect children from viewing inappropriate programs. It is not the government's job to control what children watch.

In 1988, Congressman Peter Rodino spoke of censorship as dangerous. He said Congress must be a "protector of commerce."

Jack Valenti is the head of the Motion Picture Association of America. He is against censorship of movies. "Where do we draw the line?" he said. Who would decide what should and should not be banned? He is concerned that if Americans allow their art to be controlled, it will only be a matter of time before the government takes away other rights.

7

VALUES

A value is a quality held in high regard by a society. The story of John and Julie is about a child who was influenced by what he saw on television. The story is also about values.

John was very young. He was learning about right and wrong. He was developing a sense of who he was. He was figuring out what was real and what was pretend. Perhaps he was too young to understand everything that he did. Yet he felt responsible for his actions.

The values that influenced John were from a television show about a teenager who had not learned important values. Loudmouth set fires as a solution to his anger. He had no respect for adults, including his parents. His family did not matter to him. He made fun of everything and everyone different from him. He tricked his parents and got away with things he knew he should not be doing. He laughed when he set his sister's bed on fire.

The producers and writers of that show influenced John. They used the cartoon about Loudmouth in a way that was damaging to at least one family. Should they continue to have the cartoon character do the same types of behaviors and influence other children?

Animation is often used in advertising. Above are the famous California Raisins. The commercial was so successful, there were reports of children asking for raisin costumes. The proven effectiveness of TV advertising is overwhelming.

8

YOUR TURN

You've read about how the media influenced one boy. You've read some facts about the media. You've also read basic arguments for and against controlling the media. Not it's your turn to voice your opinion. What do you think about violence in the media? Do you think the government should control what you see on television or read in the newspaper? On the next page are some points to think about either alone or in a group. With each point, be creative in your problem solving.

1. From the list below, select a topic that interests you.

•Cigarette use
•Alcohol use
•Violence
•Sex
•Intact families versus broken families
•Women acting weak or unintelligent
•Women acting strong or intelligent
•Men acting weak or unintelligent
•Men acting strong or intelligent

Take a piece of paper and a pen or pencil and write your topic on the top. Then draw a line down the middle of the paper, separating it into two columns. Watch one hour of television during the hours of 3 p.m. and 6 p.m. (These hours are usually devoted to programming for children and young adults.) On the left side of the paper, make a mark every time you see an example or hear a mention of your topic. Include the contents of commercials as well as programs.

With an adult's supervision, watch one hour of television during the hours of 8 p.m. and 10 p.m. (These hours are usually devoted to programming for adults.) On the right side of your paper, make a mark every time your topic appears.

At the end of your experiment, compare the totals. Which time slot had more instances of your topic? Why do you think this happened?

2. People who are more aware of how advertisers promote drugs, alcohol, toys, and foods are less likely to be influenced by their messages. Advertisers who create ads for TV, radio, newspapers, and magazines often send hidden messages. They want you to believe that using their product will help you. Sometimes these messages are real.

They are based on facts. Sometimes these messages are not real. They are based on imaginary ideas called myths.

Keep an "Advertisement Journal" to discover how many ads you really see in one week. You'll need a sheet of paper and a pen or pencil. For one week, keep an eye out for messages promoting beer, cigarettes, alcohol, fatty or junk foods, or toys. Whenever you spot one, make a journal entry. Write down where or when you saw the ad and the product the ad was promoting. Include the message the ad tried to make you believe.

Pay special attention to ads geared to children and teenagers. Include things you see on television or billboards, things you hear in song lyrics, and things you read in newspapers and magazines.

3. Divide a sheet of paper into two columns. Label the left column "Advertising Myths." Label the right "Advertising Realities." Use your journal entries from the second exercise to find the messages advertisers tried to promote. Write the message under the column for myth or reality. If the message is a myth, write a more realistic truth about the product.

For example, in your journal entry you may have written about a toy commercial you saw on TV. The commercial may have shown the toy with real people, exploding volcanoes, and falling rocks. The actual toy, however, may be a quiet board game. The hidden message of the ad may be, "If you play this game, you will see volcanoes explode and rocks falling." Is that a myth or a reality? What other message might this example send?

4. Ask your teacher and principal for permission to conduct a scientific experiment at a nearby grade school. Arrange to visit a class of kindergarten children in your school district.

For your experiment you'll need: ribbons of three different colors (at least ten to twelve of each color); a ten-minute cartoon showing hitting, punching, shooting, or similar acts of violence; a ten-minute cartoon about love and caring; pens and paper for your class.

Separate the kindergarten group into three smaller groups. Assign a color ribbon to each group and attach the ribbons to each group member. Take one group into another room and show them the violent cartoon. Take the second group into another room and show them the loving and caring cartoon. Do not show the third group any cartoon.

Give the kindergartners free time to play creatively within their own group. Tell each group that this is a great time to use their imaginations. At the end of ten minutes, bring all three groups out to the playground to play together. Let them play together for 20 minutes while you and your class observe their behavior. Write down every time you see any sign of aggression or violence. Note what color group the child belonged in.

When you return to your class, compare your findings with your classmates. What differences did you find among the three groups of children? Draw your own conclusions about television violence from your observations.

5. How does the media influence you? You can find out by keeping a journal of programs you watch in one week. Every time you watch television, keep track of the time you spent and the programs you watched. Mark down how many hours the television was on in the house, even if you were not watching it.

Write in your journal how you felt after watching different shows. What products did you want to buy? Did you change your opinion about a topic after watching a program? Think about what else you might have been doing if you were not watching television. Did you ever push the off button because the program bothered you in any way? Why or why not?

GLOSSARY

Aggression: starting fights or attacking others, often for no reason.

Censor: a person who reads literature or views art and films and decides if it is suitable for others to see or read.

Censorship: the removal of something from films or literature by a censor.

Children Viewing Hours: hours when television is most likely to be seen by children; usually before 7 p.m.

Hate Crimes: acts committed in anger without regard to the value of human life, pain, or suffering.

Intoxication: the state of being drunk from too much alcohol; comes from the word "toxic" which means poison.

Monitor: to keep track of what is going on.

Obesity: a state of being very ~~fat.~~ *overwieght*

Prime-time: hours that television has the most adult viewers; usually between 8 p.m. and 11 p.m.

Regulate: to control.

Index

For Further Reading

•*Mind and Media: The Effects of Television, Video Games and Computers* by Patricia Marks Greenfield, Cambridge MA, Harvard University Press, 1984.

•*Violence and the Media* by Gilda Berger, New York, Franklin Watts, 1989.

ABOUT THE AUTHOR

Dr. Cynthia DiLaura Devore, a pediatrician specializing in school health, is a former special educator and speech pathologist. Her role as a school physician blends her training and experience in both education and medicine. She is the author of a series of books for children covering issues of loss and separation. That series, Children of Courage, is available through Abdo and Daughters. Dr. Devore lives in Rochester, New York, with her husband and two sons.